In honor of Pirot Utong

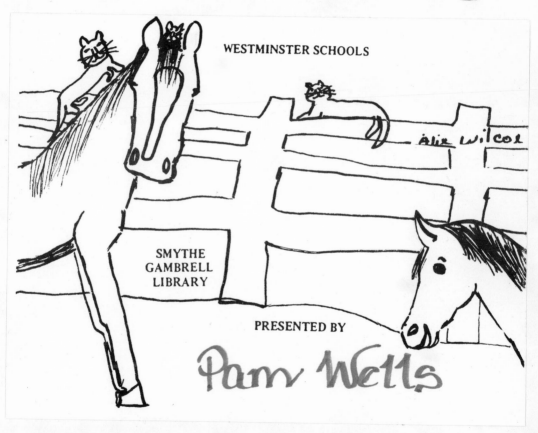

WESTMINSTER SCHOOLS

Alie Wilcox

SMYTHE
GAMBRELL
LIBRARY

PRESENTED BY

Pam Wells

A New True Book

ANTARCTICA

By Lynn M. Stone

CHILDRENS PRESS ®

CHICAGO

Tour boat enters the Lemaire Channel in Antarctica.

PHOTO CREDITS

Tom Stack and Associates
© S. Chester—2, 10 (right), 16 (2 photos), 32 (right)
© Kevin Schafer—cover, 6 (right), 15, 32 (left)
© M.P. Kahl—9, 24 (left), 31 (left), 34 (2 photos), 35, 36 (left), 42 (right)
© Shabica—19
© W. Perry Conway—20
© Bruce M. Wellman—22 (left)
© Rod Allin—22 (right)

Roloc Color Slides—6 (left), 29 (left), 44 (left)

Root Resources
© W. Helfrich—10 (left), 11, 24 (right), 26 (left), 27, 31 (right), 39 (right), 45

Emilie Lepthien—13, 26 (right), 29 (right), 43 (2 photos), 44 (right)

Historical Pictures Service, Chicago—23, 39 (left), 41 (2 photos), 42 (left)

Lynn Stone—36 (right)

Australian Information Service—37

John Forsberg—4

Len Meents—21

Cover: U.S. Coast Guard cutter *Polar Star* in McMurdo Sound, Antarctica

Library of Congress Cataloging in Publication Data

Stone, Lynn M.
  Antarctica.

  (A New true book)
  Includes index.
    1. Natural history—Antarctic Regions—Juvenile
literature. 2. Antarctic Regions—Juvenile literature.
I. Title.
QH84.1.S759   1985   508.98'9   85-5956
ISBN 0-516-01265-7   AACR2

TABLE OF CONTENTS

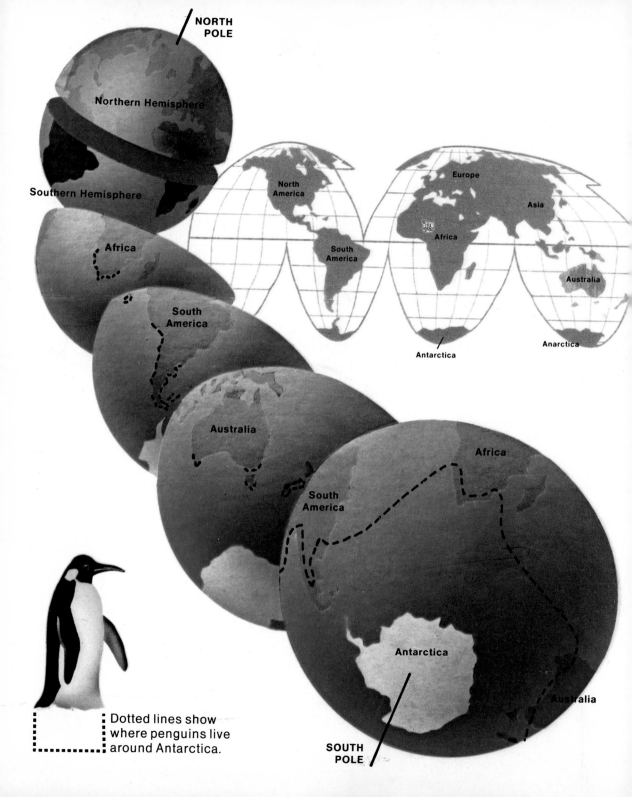

NORTH POLE

Northern Hemisphere

Southern Hemisphere

Africa

South America

Australia

Antarctica

SOUTH POLE

North America

South America

Europe

Asia

Africa

Australia

Anarctica

Antarctica

Africa

South America

Australia

Dotted lines show where penguins live around Antarctica.

FINDING ANTARCTICA

There are seven continents on our planet Earth. A continent is a great area of land. Six of the continents are North America, South America, Europe, Africa, Asia, and Australia.

The seventh continent is Antarctica. It lies at the southern tip of the world.

Hallett Station (left). Pack ice in McMurdo Sound (right)

Like the other continents, Antarctica is a huge mass of land. It is the size of Europe and the United States together. Antarctica is one of the world's largest pieces of land.

THE CONTINENT

Antarctica is not like the other continents. It is the coldest, windiest, and iciest place on earth.

Antarctica is a white continent. Most of it is covered with ice and snow.

The wind can blow up to two hundred miles per hour—twice as hard as a hurricane blows! When the wind blows the snow, the sky and the ground look alike. Antarctica explorers call this a whiteout.

Very little snow falls in Antarctica. But the snow that does fall slowly turns to ice because the air is so cold. In some places the ice and snow are more than two miles deep!

In winter the temperature may fall to minus 100 degrees Fahrenheit. One day in 1960 the

Ice cave

temperature dropped to
minus 126.9 degrees
Fahrenheit, a world record.
Travel in Antarctica is
difficult. Antarctica is cold,

Glaciers (left) and mountains make travel in Antarctica difficult.

windy, and full of
mountains. Between the
mountains are steep
valleys and rivers of ice
called glaciers.

During midwinter the sun
never rises in Antarctica.
The continent is nearly

The sun does not drop below the horizon in summer.

dark twenty-four hours a day. In midsummer there is daylight around the clock. But this does not make Antarctica warm. It remains so cold that plants and animals cannot live on most of the continent.

A LAND WITHOUT PEOPLE

Thousands of years ago, Eskimos settled in the Arctic at the northern tip of the world.

But Antarctica has never had a people of its own. Antarctica is so cold that people could not live there.

There are no cities in Antarctica. Most of the people who visit there are scientists. They study the

Palmer Station on Anvers Island is operated by the United States.

winds, temperatures, rocks,
wildlife, and ice cover.

No country owns
Antarctica. Many countries
are interested in it,
however. But a treaty
keeps Antarctica from
being owned by anyone.

ANTARCTIC OCEANS

The Antarctic continent is surrounded by oceans. The Atlantic, Pacific, and Indian oceans all touch Antarctica.

Salt water—the kind of water in oceans—does not usually freeze. But the air and water around Antarctica are so cold that the ocean water forms ice. Even the salt and the ocean currents cannot keep the water from freezing.

United States Coast Guard cutter, the *Polar Star,* breaks through the ice at McMurdo Sound.

In winter, the ice in the ocean may cover an area almost as large as the continent. Close to Antarctica the ice makes a solid ring. Farther north, the ice is loose.

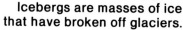
Icebergs are masses of ice
that have broken off glaciers.

In October, rising
temperatures and strong
winds break up the ice.
Huge chunks of ice called
icebergs are everywhere.
Special ships called
icebreakers can then ram
through the ring of broken
ice and reach Antarctica.

PLANTS AND ANIMALS

Because most of Antarctica is covered with ice, almost nothing can live on it. There are no trees or shrubs and only three kinds of flowering plants.

The only animals that live on Antarctica all year long are insects, spiders, and other small creatures. Antarctica's largest animal is a fly without wings. It is smaller than a housefly!

North of the continent are several small islands. They are warmer than Antarctica, and have much more plant and animal life. This area is called subantarctica.

The oceans around Antarctica are full of tiny plants. They are too small to see without a microscope. But they are big enough to be food for tiny animals.

Enlarged picture of krill

The most important of
these tiny sea animals are
krill. Krill have soft shells.
They look like shrimp.

19

Blue whales eat krill.

Krill eat the tiny plants. Seabirds, seals, and whales eat krill. Some krill are also caught by people. Someday krill may be used as food in many countries.

WHALES

The blue whale is the biggest animal in the Antarctica region. It is the largest animal that has ever lived. Its appetite is tremendous. The blue whale eats three tons—six thousand pounds—of krill each day.

Horse

Blue Whale

Humpback whales

Humpback, sperm,
finback, and bottle-nosed
whales eat krill, too.
Whales like the Antarctic
oceans because food is
easy to find.

Whales used to be
plentiful in the Antarctic.
Then whale hunters sailed

Early whale hunters

into the region and killed
most of them.

The early whale hunters
harpooned whales from
ships. Then they towed the
whales to little villages
north of Antarctica. Whale
fat, called blubber, was
melted. The oil from the
blubber was used for fuel.

Deserted whaling station (left) and a pile of whale bones (right)
are reminders of the thousands of animals killed by whale hunters.

Later, hunters killed millions
of seals and penguins
for their fat.

When hunting stopped,
the seals and the penguins
came back. But the
whales, still hunted by only
a few nations, are now rare.

SEALS

Several kinds of seals are found in the Antarctic.

The Ross seal is named for James Ross, an English explorer. Like all seals, the Ross seal is very quick under water. It catches fish with its sharp teeth.

There are several thousand Ross seals, but there are around sixteen million crabeater seals.

Leopard seal (left) and crabeater seal (right)

Actually, the crabeater seal
is not a crab eater—it is a
krill eater!

The leopard seal is a
long, sleek seal. It is quite
fierce. It eats penguins and
other seals, as well as krill.
It has even been known to
attack Antarctic explorers.

Weddell seal

The Weddell seal is the
only seal that spends the
winter near Antarctica. It
stays underwater most of
the time.

The below-zero winter air
is too cold for the Weddell
seal. But the water under
the ice is much warmer,
about 29 degrees Fahrenheit.

The Weddell seal often

stays underwater for half an hour or more. Finally it has to poke its head up to breathe. The seal uses its teeth and its thousand-pound body to keep an open hole in the ice. If it doesn't, it drowns.

The southern elephant seal lives in the seas north of Antarctica. It can weigh up to five thousand pounds!

Elephant seals and Antarctic fur seals were

Only the male elephant seal
(left) has a big nose. The females
(above) do not have big noses.

almost wiped out by seal
hunters in the 1800s. One
of those hunters was
James Weddell. Weddell
did not help the seals of
Antarctica, but he was one
of the first to have a seal
named after him.

ANTARCTIC BIRDS

Millions of penguins live in the Antarctic.

Penguins' wings are more like flippers than wings. They help make them fine swimmers. Penguins cannot fly, but they do not need to fly. They have no enemies on land.

Emperor and Adelie penguins can slide on their bellies over ice and snow.

Millions of penguins, including
the Adelie penguins (left),
live in Antarctica.

The largest and most
remarkable penguin is the
emperor. Emperor penguins
are four feet tall and
weigh up to eighty pounds!
The female emperor
penguin lays one egg in

31

A king penguin (left) sits on its egg.
Emperor penguins (above)

winter on the Antarctic ice.
Then the male takes the
egg. He tucks it between
the tops of his feet and a
flap of skin. The skin is
like a blanket for the egg.
The female emperor
leaves the male standing

with the egg. Then she walks perhaps fifty miles to the open sea for food.

But just before the egg hatches, the female returns to her tired and hungry mate. Then the male walks to the sea. When the male returns, the female leaves again.

The baby penguin hatches in July—wintertime in Antarctica. Hurricane winds howl. The temperature is minus 75 degrees Fahrenheit or

Albatross in flight (above) and royal albatross (right)

lower. The sun does not rise. The chicks live on food coughed up by their parents.

The albatross is a sailing bird. Its long, narrow wings are perfect for gliding.

The skua, a large brown gull, eats the eggs and

Skua with a penguin egg

young of other birds. In
fact, skua eat almost
anything, including garbage.

The petrel is a small
seabird. Most petrels are
robin sized. They dart over
the seas like large

Southern giant petrel (left) and Arctic tern (right)

mosquitoes. Some nest among the rocks.

The Arctic tern is the world's champion long-distance flier. It raises its young in the Arctic, at the north tip of the world. Then it flies over ten thousand miles to Antarctica.

EXPLORATION

For a long time, people suspected there was land at the bottom of the earth. But no one had seen it.

In 1772 Captain James Cook sailed from England

Captain James Cook

to look for a southern continent. He saw ice, but he did not see Antarctica. His wooden ship *Resolution* was not strong enough to break through the ice.

Captain Cook was just 150 miles from Antarctica, but he had to turn back.

In the early 1800s, English and American ships sailed in Antarctica seas to hunt seals and whales. But they did not see the continent.

Thaddeus Bellingshausen, a Russian, finally saw land in 1820, but he did not know it was the Antarctic continent.

Lieutenant Charles Wilkes of the United States Navy sailed for 1,500 miles along the coast of

Charles Wilkes (left) explored the forbidding Antarctica coastline.

Antarctica in 1838. His trip proved that there was a southern continent.

In 1895, the crew of a Norwegian whaling ship, the *Antarctic,* made the first landing on Antarctica.

In 1911 a race began to see who would reach the South Pole first. The South Pole is the imaginary geographical center point at the bottom of the earth. It is on Antarctica.

Norwegian Roald Amundsen and his group

Roald Amundsen (left) and
Robert Scott (above)

reached the pole first, on
December 14, 1911.
Robert Scott of England
and his four men arrived
there a month later.
Amundsen made it home
safely. But Scott and his
men ran out of food and
froze to death.

Richard Byrd (left) and research station (right) set up by Argentina at Paradise Harbor

One of the most famous Antarctic explorers was an American, Richard E. Byrd. He led his first expedition in 1928. He led four more expeditions before he died in 1957.

In the 1950s many countries began to

This mountaintop cross (left) at McMurdo Naval Air Station recalls Robert Scott's heroic, but fatal, journey to the South Pole. Scott's hut (above) is surrounded by more modern structures.

construct buildings in Antarctica for scientists and some military people. The largest settlement is America's McMurdo Naval Air Station. McMurdo has a runway of ice for airplanes.

ANTARCTICA'S FUTURE

No wars have been fought in Antarctica. The continent has not been ruined. The seals and penguins have come back.

Penguins (below) and giant glaciers (right) are some of Antarctica's special sights.

Even the whales may
come back some day.

Antarctica is a place
where people from many
nations go to learn, not to
conquer. Perhaps people
will always use the great
white continent wisely.

WORDS YOU SHOULD KNOW

blubber(BLUHB • er) — whale fat used as fuel

continents(KAHNT • in • ents) — the seven major great land areas on our globe

expedition(ek • spuh • DISH • un) — a trip made for a special purpose, often to explore

explorer(ek • SPLOR • er) — a person who explores, or travels, in search of specific information or objects

Fahrenheit(FAIR • en • hite) — a temperature scale, devised by Gabriel D. Fahrenheit (1686-1736), a German scientist

glacier(GLAY • sher) — a river of ice that moves down a valley, finally reaching the sea, where it breaks into icebergs

harpoon(har • POON) — to kill a whale by throwing or shooting at it a long spear called a harpoon

iceberg(ICE • berg) — a large piece of floating ice that has broken off from a glacier

icebreaker(ICE • bray • ker) — a special ship used to break up ice to make a passageway through it for other ships

krill(KRIL) — tiny sea animals that are the main food of whales

settlement(SET • il • ment) — a place where people have settled, or taken up residence

South Pole(SOWTH POHL) — a geographical imaginary place that is the southernmost spot on Earth

subantarctica(sub • ant • ARK • tih • kuh) — the region just north of Antarctica and the Antarctic Circle

treaty(TREET • ee) — an agreement made to promote peace

whiteout(WITE • owt) — a condition of weather when blowing snow makes the sky and the ground look alike and it is difficult to travel

INDEX

About the Author

Lynn M. Stone was born and raised in Meridan, Connecticut. He received his undergraduate degree from Aurora College in Illinois and his master's degree from Northern Illinois University. Once a teacher in Sarasota, Florida, Mr. Stone currently teaches English to junior high school students in the West Aurora Public School system.

A freelance wildlife photographer and journalist, Lynn has had his work appear in many publications including National Wildlife, Ranger Rick, Oceans, Country Gentlemen, Animal Kingdom, *and* International Wildlife. *He has also contributed to* Time-Life, National Geographic, Audubon Field Guide, *and Hallmark Cards.*

Many of Lynn Stone's photographs have been used in the New True Books published by Childrens Press.